OSBORNE

*Her Majesty's Dinner.*

Christmas Day, 1900

Potages.
Tortue claire    Crême d'orge à l'Américaine

Poissons.
Turbot sauce mousseuse
Filets de sole panés sauce Ravigote

Entrée.
Celestines à la Noël

Relèves.
Dindonneau à la Chipolata
Chine of Pork
Roast Beef    Plum Pudding

Entremets.
Asperges sauce Hollandaise
Mince Pies
Eclairs au chocolat

Buffet
Baron of Beef    Woodcock Pie    Game Pie
Boar's Head    Brawn

# VICTORIA and HER COURT

LIFE IN VICTORIAN ENGLAND

# VICTORIA and HER COURT

VIRGINIA SCHOMP

MARSHALL CAVENDISH • BENCHMARK
NEW YORK

*For MFN Taylor Schomp*

The author and publishers would like to thank Walter L. Arnstein, Professor of History Emeritus at the University of Illinois at Urbana-Champaign, for his valuable comments and careful reading of the manuscript.

Other Marshall Cavendish Offices: Marshall Cavendish International (Asia) Private Limited, 1 New Industrial Road, Singapore 536196 • Marshall Cavendish International (Thailand) Co Ltd. 253 Asoke, 12th Flr, Sukhumvit 21 Road, Klongtoey Nua, Wattana, Bangkok 10110, Thailand • Marshall Cavendish (Malaysia) Sdn Bhd, Times Subang, Lot 46, Subang Hi-Tech Industrial Park, Batu Tiga, 40000 Shah Alam, Selangor Darul Ehsan, Malaysia

Marshall Cavendish is a trademark of Times Publishing Limited
All websites were available and accurate when this book was sent to press.

LIBRARY OF CONGRESS CATALOGING-IN-PUBLICATION DATA Schomp, Virginia. Victoria and her court / by Virginia Schomp. p. cm. — (Life in Victorian England) Includes bibliographical references and index. Summary: "A social history of Victorian England, focusing on life in the upper echelons of society during the reign of Queen Victoria (1837-1901)"—Provided by publisher. ISBN 978-1-60870-028-8 1. Victoria, Queen of Great Britain, 1819-1901—Relations with courts and courtiers—Juvenile literature. 2. Great Britain—Court and courtiers—History—19th century—Juvenile literature. 3. Aristocracy (Social class)—Great Britain—History—19th century—Juvenile literature. 4. Great Britain—Politics and government—1837-1901—Juvenile literature. I. Title. DA559.5.S36 2010 941.081092—dc22 2009029688

EDITOR: Joyce Stanton PUBLISHER: Michelle Bisson ART DIRECTOR: Anahid Hamparian SERIES DESIGNER: Michael Nelson

Images provided by Rose Corbett Gordon, Art Editor of Mystic CT, from the following sources: Cover: The Art Archive/Musée du Château de Versailles/Gianni Dagli Orti Back cover: Hulton Archive/Getty Images Page 1: The Art Archive/Lord Edward Pelham Clinton Collection; pages 2-3: The Art Archive/Bibliothèque des Arts Décoratifs Paris/Gianni Dagli Orti; pages 7, 8: Tate, London/Art Resource, NY; page 11: The Art Archive/Private Collection/Eileen Tweedy; page 12: Fine Arts Photographic Library/Corbis; page 15: The Art Archive/Musée du Château de Versailles/Gianni Dagli Orti; page 17: The Francis Firth Collection/Corbis; page 19: Private Collection/Bridgeman Art Library; pages 22, 64: Historical Picture Archives/Corbis; page 24: Stapleton Collection/Corbis; pages 26, 52, 66: The Art Archive; page 27: Erich Lessing/Art Resource, NY; page 29: Hulton-Deutsch Collection/Corbis; page 30: The Art Archive/Private Collection; page 32: The Art Archive/Miramare Museum Trieste/Alfredo Dagli Orti; page 35: Adoc-photos/Art Resource, NY; pages 37, 59: Bettmann/Corbis; page 38: Corbis; page 39: Chris Hellier/Corbis; pages 41, 55, 72: Hulton Archive/Getty Images; page 42: Mary Evans Picture Library/The Image Works; page 44: Ipswich Borough Council Museums and Galleries, Suffolk, UK/Bridgeman Art Library; page 46: C.P. Koepke ©TopFoto/The Image Works; page 47: TopFoto/The Image Works; page 51: Museum of London/Bridgeman Art Library; page 60: Private Collection/© Philip Gale Fine Art, Chepstow, Gwent, Wales, UK/Bridgeman Art Library; page 62: The Art Archive/Victoria and Albert Museum/Sally Chappell; page 68: The Art Archive/John Meek.

Printed in Malaysia (T)
135642

*Front cover:* A portrait of Queen Victoria as a young woman
*Half-title page:* The menu for a lavish Christmas dinner at one of the queen's private residences, Osborne House
*Title page:* Noble subjects honor the queen on the fiftieth anniversary of her rule.
*Back cover:* Victoria's youngest son, Leopold

# CONTENTS

# ABOUT VICTORIAN ENGLAND

ON JUNE 20, 1837, KING WILLIAM IV OF ENGLAND DIED, and his eighteen-year-old niece, Victoria, ascended the throne. The teenage queen recorded her thoughts in her diary:

> Since it has pleased Providence to place me in this station, I shall do my utmost to fulfil my duty towards my country; I am very young and perhaps in many, though not in all things, inexperienced, but I am sure, that very few have more real good will and more real desire to do what is fit and right than I have.

That blend of faith, confidence, devotion to duty, and the earnest desire to do good would guide Victoria through the next sixty-three years and seven months, the longest reign of any English monarch. The queen's personal qualities would also set the tone for the period that bears her name, the Victorian Age.

Today the term *Victorian* is sometimes used to describe someone who is prim and prudish. We may think of Queen Victoria as a stuffy old lady presiding over a long, formal dinner party where everyone watches their language and worries about which fork to use. That image is not entirely wrong. Victoria *was* an old-fashioned person who believed in "traditional values" such as duty, discipline, and self-control. Victorian society *was* governed by a set of strict moral and social rules. However, that is not the whole picture. When we look deeper, we discover that the queen was also a passionate woman who loved music, dancing, and laughter. Her long reign, far from being dull and predictable, was a period of extraordinary growth and change. Between 1837 and 1901, England was transformed from a mostly agricultural, isolated society into a modern industrial nation

Three elegant young ladies play cards, in a painting by the popular Victorian artist John Everett Millais.

with territories all over the world. The Victorian people witnessed astonishing advances in science and technology, as well as sweeping political, legal, and social reforms. A Victorian physician named Sir Henry Holland described his exciting times as "an age of transition, a period when changes, deeply and permanently affecting the whole condition of mankind, are occurring more rapidly, as well as extensively, than at any prior time in human history."

*Life in Victorian England* takes a look at this dynamic era, with a focus on the people and their everyday lives. The four books in the series will introduce us to men, women, and children at all levels of society, from poor farmers and factory workers to thriving middle-class families to the aristocrats at the top of the social scale. In this volume we will meet the leaders of government, the lords and ladies of Victoria's court, and the queen herself. We will see where these privileged people lived and worked, how they celebrated special occasions, and how they coped with the challenges of their times.

Now it is time to step back to a world that is poised on the brink of the modern age. Welcome to an era when gas lamps are giving way to electric lightbulbs, stagecoaches to locomotives, wooden sailing vessels to iron warships. Welcome to life in Victorian England!

Eighteen-year-old Victoria receives the news of her ascension to the throne.

## ONE

# VICTORIA'S EMPIRE

We seem, as it were, to have conquered and peopled
half the world in a fit of absence of mind.
~ Sir John Seeley, "The Expansion of England" (1883)

THERE WERE NO PUBLIC OPINION POLLS BACK IN 1837, when Victoria became queen. If there had been, the headlines in British newspapers might have read: MONARCHY'S APPROVAL RATINGS AT ALL-TIME LOW.

The problem was part political, part personal. During the preceding decades, the public's respect for the monarchy had gradually declined as the power of Britain's national legislature rose. At the same time, the royal family had been mired in one scandal after another. Victoria's father had enjoyed a lavish lifestyle that left him deeply in debt. Her uncles, including King William IV, had built up reputations for idleness, extravagance, and other excesses. The British were sick and tired of the undignified behavior of the "wicked royals."

Some people even thought that the country should do away with the monarchy altogether.

Then eighteen-year-old Victoria inherited the throne. To the British, the lovely "girl-queen" seemed like a breath of spring after a long, chilly winter. The wife of an American diplomat living in England observed that the entire country was "run mad with loyalty to the young Queen. . . . Nothing is talked about but her beauty, her wisdom, her gentleness, . . . her goodness."

The praise only grew louder as the new queen set about repairing the monarchy's tarnished image. Victoria believed in hard work, thrift, honesty, self-discipline, and devotion to country. In the years to come, she would strive to make the royal family a living example of those virtues. Her efforts would help preserve the monarchy, while providing her subjects with stability and reassurance in tumultuous times.

## TO REIGN, NOT TO RULE

Victoria was not the kind of ruler who could run a kingdom with a wave of her royal hand. By the time she became queen, Britain was a constitutional monarchy. In that form of government, the monarch is the formal head of state, but his or her powers are strictly limited by the country's constitution. As a nineteenth-century British writer put it, the king or queen "reigns but does not rule."

Who did "rule" over Victorian England? Since the early 1800s, the day-to-day business of governing had been the responsibility of Parliament and the prime minister. Parliament was Great Britain's national legislature. It had two branches: the House of Lords, made up mainly of high-ranking nobles who inherited their "seats"; and the House of Commons, comprised of elected representatives. Two political parties dominated Parliament, the Tories (later known as the Conservatives) and the Whigs (or Liberals). The prime minister was

the leader of the party with the most seats in the House of Commons. He appointed a cabinet of officials (also called "ministers") to advise him and oversee the government departments.

While the monarch did not actually run the country, he or she was far from powerless. Under British laws and traditions, Queen Victoria was kept informed of all government business. She had the right to see all important government documents and to be consulted before major policy changes and cabinet appointments. She received regular briefings from the prime minister, and she was expected to tell him when she disagreed with the course government was taking. She even had the power to nominate a new prime minister at times when no political party had a clear majority in the House of Commons.

From the start of her reign, Victoria took these duties seriously. She met often with her prime minister and other top officials. She spent many hours each day reviewing government reports and signing official papers. Far from complaining about the dull side of her work, the youthful queen raved, "I get so many papers to sign every day, that I have always a very great deal to do; . . . I delight in this work."

The queen arrives at London's Westminster Palace for the annual ceremony marking the opening of Parliament.

VICTORIA'S EMPIRE

11

# ROYAL RIGHTS AND POWERS

In 1867 the British journalist Walter Bagehot (pronounced *BADGE-utt*) wrote what would become the most widely read book on the British system of government. *The English Constitution* examined the complicated British Constitution, which is not a single written document but a body of accumulated laws and traditions. It analyzed the constitutional powers of Parliament, the prime minister, and the monarch. Bagehot also took a look at the considerable behind-the-scenes influence of the king or queen.

*Above*: Victoria consults with one of her favorite prime ministers, Benjamin Disraeli.

The use of the Queen, in a dignified capacity, is incalculable. Without her in England, the present English Government would fail and pass away. . . .

The first Minister [prime minister], it is understood, transmits to her authentic information of all the most important decisions, together with . . . the more important votes in Parliament. He is bound to take care that she knows everything which there is to know as to the passing politics of the nation. She has by rigid usage the right to complain if she does not know of every great act of her Ministry, not only before it is done, but while there is yet time to consider it—while it is still possible that it may not be done.

To state the matter shortly, the sovereign has, under a constitutional monarchy such as ours, three rights—the right to be consulted, the right to encourage, the right to warn. And a king of great sense and sagacity [wisdom] would want no others. He would find that his having no others would enable him to use these with singular effect. He would say to his Minister: "The responsibility of these measures is upon you. Whatever you think best must be done. Whatever you think best shall have my full and effectual support. *But* you will observe that for this reason and that reason what you propose to do is bad; for this reason and that reason what you do not propose is better. I do not oppose, it is my duty not to oppose; but observe that I *warn*." Supposing the king to be right, and to have what kings often have, the gift of effectual expression, he could not help moving his Minister.

## "OUR CIVILIZING MISSION"

When Victoria came to the throne, she received an impressive title: Queen of the United Kingdom of Great Britain and Ireland. The kingdom that she inherited encompassed the four countries of the British Isles: England, Scotland, Wales, and Ireland.* She also became queen of a hodgepodge of colonies and territories scattered all over the globe.

Watching over this far-flung empire was the strongest navy in the world. The Royal Navy battled slave traders. (Parliament had abolished the slave trade in the British Empire in 1807.) It fought wars and protected Britain from foreign aggression. Just as importantly, its great fleet of wooden warships guarded the nation's highly profitable trade routes.

Britain's growth as a trading power had been made possible by the Industrial Revolution. The shift from an agricultural economy to one based on large-scale factory production began in England in the mid- to late 1700s. Soon British ships were crisscrossing the oceans, carrying inexpensive manufactured goods to foreign lands and returning with raw materials for the factories at home. By 1830, Great Britain controlled nearly half of all world trade.

Trade was also the driving force behind the early growth of the British Empire. In order to protect its commercial interests, a privately owned British trading company called the East India Company had taken over much of India, making it the largest of the empire's colonies. British naval bases, trading posts, and colonies had also

---

*The British Isles are two islands off the coast of western Europe. The larger island, called Great Britain, contains England, Scotland, and Wales. In 1801 these three countries joined together with the neighboring island-nation of Ireland to form the United Kingdom of Great Britain and Ireland. In everyday speech, both in Victorian times and today, people often have used "England" or "Britain" to refer to the island of Great Britain or to the whole United Kingdom.

sprung up in Australia, New Zealand, Canada, the West Indies, southern Africa, and other widely separated lands. (These included the profitable but troublesome American colonies, which won their independence in 1783.)

The British Empire continued to grow by fits and starts during Victoria's reign. The most frenzied period of expansion began in the 1880s, with the brutal "Scramble for Africa." Other European powers were competing for control of the African continent, with its rich raw materials and markets. Great Britain jumped tooth and claw into the fray and emerged with the lion's share. British forces secured territories all over the continent, sometimes with promises and treaties, sometimes with rifles and machine guns. British colonial governments would eventually rule over nearly a third of Africa's population.

The Victorians did not think of themselves as conquerors. In their eyes, they were an enlightened people bringing civilization to a backward world. Nowhere was that crusading spirit more evident than in Africa. Religious societies financed expeditions to the continent, with the aim of spreading Christianity and suppressing the slave trade. Missionaries founded schools, churches, and medical clinics. In 1896, when British forces occupied Nigeria, a London magazine printed a picture of African princes swearing an oath to renounce slavery. The caption read: "Here we see our civilizing mission in action."

By the end of the nineteenth century, Britain ruled over the largest empire the world has ever known. More than four hundred million people lived under some form of British rule. A quarter of the globe flew the British flag. The Victorian people could declare with pride: "The sun never sets on the British Empire."

## RICH MAN, POOR MAN

The people who built the British Empire were born into a society that had long been divided into two classes: aristocrats and commoners. The aristocrats were the privileged minority who inherited titles and great estates. The commoners included everyone else.

In actual practice there were *three* levels of British society, each with its own internal rankings of income and importance. At the bottom of the social scale were members of the lower classes, who made up about three-quarters of the population. Lower-class people included farmers, servants, skilled and unskilled workers in various trades, and ever-increasing numbers of factory workers.

Next came the middle class. This group grew steadily during the Victorian Age, eventually reaching about one-quarter of the population. It embraced a wide range of occupations and income levels, from lower-middle-class clerks to more prosperous merchants, doctors, and lawyers, all the way to wealthy bankers and industrialists.

The people of the upper class owned nearly all the land in Britain. Land was passed down from generation to generation, usually from a father to his eldest son. Most estates were carved into parcels and rented out to farmers, earning both income and power for the landowners.

A barefoot boy sells matches on the streets of Victorian London.

There were two distinct groups within the upper class: the landed gentry and the aristocrats. In Victorian times there were about 2,000 landed gentlemen, who owned estates averaging from one thousand to three thousand acres. The gentry were important and respected people in their local communities. The aristocrats, who inherited prestigious titles along with their money and estates, were even more highly honored. In the early 1840s, there were about 560 titled families in England, with lands that often extended over thousands of acres. Ranked from highest to lowest, the titles of these great nobles, or "peers," were duke/duchess, marquess/marchioness, earl/countess, viscount/viscountess, and baron/baroness.

Over the centuries few Britons ever dreamed of challenging this traditional class system. Everyone knew his or her place in the social order and was expected to stick to it. The words of a popular hymn written in the 1840s summed up the social climate:

All things bright and beautiful,
All creatures great and small,
All things wise and wonderful,
The Lord God made them all. . . .

The rich man in his castle,
The poor man at his gate,
God made them, high or lowly,
And order'd their estate.

## AN AGE OF REFORMS

The Industrial Revolution did more than change the way people manufactured goods. It also transformed society. At the start of Victoria's reign, Britain was still essentially a rural nation, but more and more people were moving from farms and villages to the cities where factories were located. In 1801 only 20 percent of the population of Great Britain had lived in cities. By the end of the century, that figure would soar to nearly 80 percent.

At the same time, the overall population was booming. Between 1801 and 1841, the number of people in Great Britain nearly doubled, from about 11 million to 19 million. As a large portion of this population poured into London, Liverpool, Manchester, and other manufacturing cities, conditions quickly went from bad to horrible. Men, women, and children were crowded together in filthy, run-down housing, with little light or ventilation and no indoor plumbing. Factories polluted the air and water. The streets often ran with raw sewage.

Millions of poor and working-class Victorians were forced to live in dark, dirty, over-crowded city slums.

While the lower classes struggled, the middle class was slowly becoming more prosperous. Well-paying jobs were opening up in industry, finance, and government for those with even a modest education. Doctors, lawyers, and other professionals were gaining new respect and influence. The most successful bankers and manufacturers were amassing gigantic fortunes.

All these social changes led to sweeping transformations in the political system, too. The aristocrats and landed gentry had always kept a tight hold on the reins of British government. The head of a titled family was automatically a member of the House of Lords. Only men who owned a certain amount of property could vote in elections or serve in the House of Commons. Now members of the rising middle class began to demand a greater voice in government. Lower-class workers began to organize, demanding higher wages, better working and living conditions, and improved government services.

The first significant change came five years before the start of Victoria's reign. The Reform Act of 1832 increased city dwellers' representation in Parliament and reduced the amount of property a man had to own in order to vote. Parliament would pass several other reform measures during the Victorian period. These would include laws extending voting rights to nearly all working men and introducing the secret ballot. Gradually, Britain's old political order would give way to a more democratic society.

Queen Victoria was not always happy with these changes. On the one hand, she was sympathetic to the plight of the poor. She pushed for measures improving housing and education. She argued that "the lower classes . . . earn their bread and riches so deservedly—that they cannot and ought not to be kept back—to be abused by the wretched, ignorant, high-born beings who [live] only to kill time." On the other hand, the queen firmly opposed any movement toward republicanism, which would mean the abolition of the monarchy. In a letter to a daughter living in Prussia, the queen vowed that she would

> yield to none in true liberalism, but republicanism and destructiveness are no true liberalism. . . . [Reform is] right and well—when fundamental landmarks are not abolished and swept away, and every good thing changed for change's sake. . . . There is the danger. If you lived here and saw and understood all that goes on you would see that these so-called, but not really "liberal" ideas are very mischievous.

The magnificent Grand Staircase at Windsor Castle was designed during the reign of Queen Victoria.

# TWO

# SPLENDID PALACES *and* "COZY" RETREATS

At a quarter-past seven o'clock we arrived at dear Balmoral. . . .
The house is charming; the rooms delightful;
the furniture, papers, everything perfection.
～QUEEN VICTORIA (SEPTEMBER 7, 1855)

THE HOMES OF BRITISH ARISTOCRATS WERE A SHARP contrast to the dwellings of the poor. While the lower classes lived in humble country cottages or squalid city apartments, the richest Victorians owned huge mansions, some with as many as thirty bedrooms. Most aristocrats had both a house in London and one or more extensive country estates.

Not surprisingly, some of the finest residences in Great Britain were associated with the royal family. When Victoria took the throne, she inherited palaces that had been built by earlier monarchs as family homes and centers of government. During her reign, she also built private residences to serve as peaceful havens away from the formality of court life.

## TWO ROYAL RESIDENCES

"I really and truly go into Buckingham Palace the day after to-morrow," Victoria wrote three weeks after becoming queen. Located in the heart of London, Buckingham Palace was one of several royal residences owned by the state and reserved for the use of the royal family. Victoria's grandfather, George III, had bought the mansion known as Buckingham House as a wedding gift for his bride. The two sons who succeeded him as king—George IV and William IV— had spent a small fortune in government funds transforming the mansion into an even more glorious palace. William died shortly before the grand project was completed. When his niece decided to make the palace her home, an army of workers had to scramble to make it ready. In July 1837 Victoria moved in, becoming the first monarch to live in the building that has been the official residence of British kings and queens ever since.

Victoria expanded Buckingham Palace, adding the large east wing that would become the "public face" of the palace.

Young Victoria was delighted with Buckingham. She adored the grand halls and music rooms, the ornately carved ceilings, the vast gardens where her pet spaniel, Dash, could play. During her first few months as queen, she brought the palace to life with an endless round of dinner parties, receptions, and balls. At the start of her first state ball, she felt "a little shy," but she was soon "so happy and so merry" that she didn't climb back up the marble staircase till four in the morning.

The queen was not as pleased with her other great royal residence, Windsor Castle. Windsor was the largest and one of the oldest castles in all of Europe. Ever since its construction in the eleventh century, it had been the home of nearly every British monarch. Victoria admired Windsor's looming towers and its setting in the green countryside outside London. At first, though, she did not feel as if she really belonged there. Wandering through the ancient castle in August 1837, she was haunted by memories of her uncle William, who had died within its walls. "I cannot help feeling as though I were not the Mistress of the House, and as if I was to see the poor King and Queen," she wrote in the daily journal that she had kept since the age of thirteen. "There is a sadness about the whole which I must say I feel."

Before long, this gloomy mood lifted. Family and friends came to stay, warming the old stone fortress with life and laughter. Victoria enjoyed playing cards and chess with the visiting lords and ladies. The long corridors were perfect for ball games with their children. Her favorite pastime, though, was horseback riding. Dressed in a long velvet riding costume, she would gallop over the countryside accompanied by dozens of riders. When it was time to return to Buckingham Palace in the fall, she was "very sorry indeed" to leave Windsor. "I passed such a very pleasant time here; the pleasantest

Queen Victoria and Prince Albert confer with the librarian in the Royal Library at Windsor Castle.

summer I ever passed in my life, and I shall never forget this first summer of my Reign."

## A "PERFECT LITTLE PARADISE"

A palace or castle might be splendid, but it could never be truly "homey." As time passed, Victoria became increasingly aware of the disadvantages of her royal residences. This was especially true after she married in 1840. Within five years, she and her husband, Prince Albert, had four children and another on the way. Buckingham Palace, their main residence, had not been built with a growing family in mind. The only place for the children's nursery was an attic originally intended as servants' quarters. Most of the palace's fireplaces did not work, and the rooms could be icy cold. The sewage pipes emptied into the courtyards, onto rooftops, and even, during heavy rains, into the kitchen. Albert denounced the building as "a disgrace to the Sovereign and the Nation," and the queen's physician declared that the conditions were downright unhealthy.

A new wing was eventually added to the palace, along with other renovations providing more space and comfort. But Victoria still longed for a place where she could "live with my beloved Albert and our children in the quiet and retirement of private life." In 1845 her dream came true. She and Prince Albert bought Osborne House on the Isle of Wight, a small island off the south coast of England. When the old house proved too small, they built a new one on the site, complete with guest cottages, a separate house for the small army of staff and servants who traveled with the queen, and an audience room where she could meet with visiting government ministers.

Osborne House was a splendid mansion, but it was also "cozy" and "snug"—two of Victoria's favorite words. The rooms were bright and cheerful, stuffed with plain rosewood furniture, pictures, and knickknacks. The children's nursery and schoolroom were near the sitting room where their parents often sat side by side at a pair of writing tables. The grounds were an artfully designed wilderness of flowers, shrubs, and trees, opening onto the deep blue sea. Victoria could not "imagine a prettier spot—valleys and woods which would be beautiful anywhere; but all this near the sea . . . is quite perfection."

The sitting area of the queen's bedroom at Osborne House, her private estate on the Isle of Wight

SPLENDID PALACES AND "COZY" RETREATS

The best part of all was that she had paid for this "perfect little Paradise" entirely out of her own income. Osborne was "our very own," which made it "doubly nice."

## LIFE IN THE HIGHLANDS

Queen Victoria was so thrilled at having her own home that she soon decided to buy another one. During a visit to Scotland in 1842, she and Prince Albert had fallen in love with the wild and rugged Highlands region. A few years later, they bought a "pretty little castle" in the Scottish Highlands called Balmoral.

Like the old house at Osborne, Balmoral Castle was too small for the still-growing royal family, which now included seven children. Under Albert's direction, the house was torn down and completely rebuilt. The new residence looked like a cross between a medieval Scottish castle and something out of Grimm's fairy tales. Its towers, turrets, and battlements, built from gray-white granite, sparkled in the sun. Within its handsome walls were family rooms, servants' quarters, a grand ballroom, a state room for court business, and a suite for visiting ministers. The wallpaper, curtains, and chair covers were a colorful riot of Scottish tartans (plaid fabrics). To Victoria, Albert's "great taste, and the impress of his dear hand" made Balmoral the perfect home.

Not everyone shared the queen's enthusiasm. One visitor grumbled that an outbreak of "tartanitis" seemed to have infected the furnishings. A number of other guests privately complained about the chilly temperatures. Victoria was a firm believer in the advantages of fresh air. She insisted on keeping the windows open, even in the middle of winter. A visiting earl swore that his toes became frostbitten at dinner, and the czar of Russia maintained that Balmoral was colder than the wastes of Siberia.

None of these concerns dampened Victoria's delight in her Highlands hideaway. In fact, she and Albert spent the happiest days of their lives at Balmoral. They loved the peaceful hillsides where they could hike or ride all day without "seeing a single human being, nor hearing a sound excepting that of the wind." Victoria enjoyed visiting the neighboring country folk. She often went out alone, stopping at the cottages and chatting with the women. Sometimes she shared their simple meals or bought butter and eggs to take back home.

Guests pose before the picturesque towers of Balmoral Castle on a typically overcast day in northern Scotland.

Gradually, Victoria developed a yearly schedule that divided her time among her two private estates and her state residences. The royal family usually went to Balmoral in late August and stayed through much of the fall. Around November they went to Windsor Castle, where they celebrated Christmas, before moving on to Osborne House in time for New Year's. The spring and summer were divided between Windsor and Osborne, along with a holiday abroad. Then it was back to Balmoral again. In the later years of her rule, Buckingham Palace was reserved mainly for official dinners, receptions, and other special occasions.

Victoria's living style was a constant source of fascination to her subjects. Small-scale copies of Osborne House sprang up all over Britain, and Balmoral Castle set off a craze for tartans and other Scottish-inspired designs. Most of all, the queen's residences, designed as cozy settings for a far-from-ordinary couple and their children, became the Victorian ideal of the family home.

Victoria wrote glowingly about the "dear, dear Highlands, the hills, the pure air, the quiet, the retirement, the liberty."

# A HIGHLANDS EXPEDITION

One of Victoria's greatest pleasures was rambling about the countryside like an "ordinary" person. In the following passage from her daily journal, she describes one such outing. The "delightful, successful expedition" took place in the fall of 1860. Victoria and Prince Albert traveled under assumed names to the Scottish village of Grantown, accompanied by Jane Churchill (one of Victoria's ladies-in-waiting), Lieutenant General Charles Grey (Albert's private secretary), and two servants, John Grant and John Brown.

Breakfasted at Balmoral in our own room at half-past seven o'clock, and started at eight or a little past, with Lady Churchill and General Grey, in the sociable [a modest horse-drawn carriage] . . . , for Castleton, where we changed horses. We went on five miles [until] we found our ponies. . . .

[The travelers rode for several miles to a ferry over the Spey River.]

Walker, the police inspector, met us, but did not keep with us. He had been sent to order everything in a quiet way, without letting people suspect who we were: in this he entirely succeeded. The ferry was a very rude [primitive] affair; . . . we could only stand on it, and it was moved at one end by two long oars, plied by the ferryman and Brown, and at the other end by a long sort of beam, which Grant took in hand. A few seconds brought us over to the road, where there were two shabby vehicles. . . . We [Victoria and Albert] had decided to call ourselves Lord and Lady Churchill and party, Lady Churchill passing as Miss Spencer, and General Grey as Dr. Grey! Brown once forgot this, and called me "Your Majesty" as I was getting into the carriage; and Grant on the box once called Albert "Your Royal Highness"; which set us off laughing, but no one observed it. . . .

On and on we went, till at length we saw lights, and drove through a long and straggling "toun," and turned down a small court to the door of the inn. . . . We went up a small staircase, and were shown to our bed-room at the top of it—very small, but clean. . . . Made ourselves "clean and tidy," and then sat down to our dinner. Grant and Brown were to have waited on us, but were "bashful" and did not. A ringletted woman did everything. . . . The dinner was very fair, and all very clean:—soup, "hodge-podge" [stew], mutton-broth with vegetables, which I did not much relish, fowl with white sauce, good roast lamb, very good potatoes, besides one or two other dishes, which I did not taste, ending with a good tart of cranberries.

Victoria married
Albert, prince of
Saxe-Coburg-Gotha,
in February 1840.

# THREE

# THE MEN
## *of*
# THE COURT

Oh! to feel I was, and am, loved by
such an Angel as Albert!

~ QUEEN VICTORIA (OCTOBER 15, 1839)

VICTORIA HAD LED A SHELTERED LIFE BEFORE SHE CAME to the throne. She had learned something about the duties and challenges of a monarch from letters exchanged with her mother's brother Leopold, king of the Belgians. Apart from her uncle's advice, however, she knew little about politics or the inner workings of the monarchy. Still, she learned her job quickly and well, with the help of several influential men.

The first and most important man behind the queen's education was the prime minister. Later, Prince Albert played a major role in shaping his wife's views. The men of the court also included a host of officeholders and servants, who helped the queen carry out her duties and ensured the smooth functioning of the royal household.

## "MY BELOVED ALBERT"

Victoria took the throne determined to do her duty—and one of a queen's most important duties was to marry and produce an heir. The most suitable candidate for a husband seemed to be her cousin Albert, prince of the tiny German state of Saxe-Coburg-Gotha. The young queen had met Albert once, and she had thought him handsome and clever. However, she was determined not to marry for several more years. She was "not yet quite grown up," she insisted. Besides, she was so used to getting her own way that "it was 10 to 1 that I shouldn't agree with any body."

All these reservations vanished on Albert's second visit to England, about two years after Victoria became queen. This time she was enraptured from the moment she laid eyes on him. The prince was "perfection in every way," from his "beautiful blue eyes" and "delicate mustachios" to his "amiable and unaffected" manners. Within five days, Albert had accepted Victoria's shy proposal. (It would have been improper for a mere prince to propose to the queen of England.) Four months later, they were married.

At the start of the marriage, Albert had no official title or duties. (He was eventually granted the title "prince consort.") In a society where a wife was expected to regard her husband as "lord and master," no one knew quite what to do with the spouse of a reigning queen. Victoria herself was reluctant to share her duties and powers with anyone, even her beloved husband. About all she would let Albert do was dry the fresh ink on her letters with blotting paper.

Over time, that began to change. In November 1840 Victoria gave birth to their first child, Princess Victoria (nicknamed Vicky). While the queen was recuperating, Albert met with her ministers and handled her official documents. Gradually, Victoria developed a keen appreciation for her husband's intelligence, good judgment, and compassion for the less fortunate. Albert became her unofficial private secretary and closest adviser. He filed her papers and kept records of her important conversations. He reviewed her ministers' reports, scoured the newspapers, and kept her up-to-date on political matters. He even wrote out letters for her signature. Under his guidance the queen became more aware of the suffering of the lower classes and more open to reforms in education, housing, and other areas. She also adopted his vision of the monarchy as a unifying force, above the fray of politics. She came to feel that she "could not exist" without Albert. As she confided in a letter to her uncle Leopold, "I should sink under the troubles and annoyances . . . of my very difficult position, were it not for his assistance, protection, guidance, and comfort."

A photo of the royal couple emphasizes their devotion, seriousness, and respectability— qualities that were greatly admired by middle-class Victorians.

Albert's health was never strong, and his long working hours often left him sick and exhausted. When he came down with a "feverish attack" in late 1861, Victoria thought that it was just another of his frequent ailments. His condition quickly worsened, and the court physicians concluded that he had typhoid fever, a serious illness most likely brought on by the unsanitary conditions at Windsor Castle. (Today many doctors believe that he may actually have had stomach cancer.) Prince Albert died on December 14, at the age of forty-two.

Victoria was devastated. She could not imagine living without the man who had become "my entire self, my very life and soul, yes even my conscience." For the next several years, she shut herself away from the world. She surrounded herself with pictures of Albert and kept his room just as he had left it. She even insisted that fresh towels and clothes be laid out for him every day. Many of her subjects admired her devotion. Just as many thought that the grieving widow had gone mad. Some newspapers called for the queen to give up the throne if she could no longer fulfill her responsibilities. It would take a powerful and persuasive prime minister to help Victoria overcome her grief and return to the land of the living.

## VICTORIA'S PRIME MINISTERS

Ten different men served as prime minister during Victoria's long reign. The first—and one of the most important—was Lord Melbourne. This brilliant politician was a fifty-eight-year-old widower grieving the recent loss of his only son when Victoria came to the throne. The task of guiding the young monarch in the first years of her reign brought new joy and purpose to his life. The queen spent hours each day with Melbourne. The prime minister shared his knowledge of British history, current political issues, and the customs, quarrels, and alliances of the aristocracy. He laced his lessons with entertaining stories about personalities past and present. Victoria found their conversations fascinating, and his witty remarks often made her laugh.

For all his dedication, there was one area in which the queen's first prime minister failed her. Lord Melbourne was the leader of the Whig Party, which favored limited democratic reforms such as the extension of voting rights. Like most members of the ruling class, however, he believed that it was not government's role to reform society. "He doubts education will ever do any good," Victoria wrote in her journal. "He is for labour and does not think the factory children are too much worked." While the young queen was sympathetic to her subjects' misfortunes, it would take Albert's influence, after Melbourne left office, to fully awaken her social conscience.

# LORD MELBOURNE

Lord Melbourne was more than a political adviser to Queen Victoria. He was also a good friend, wise teacher, and fatherly figure in the early years of her reign. The queen's journal traces the course of her relationship with the prime minister, from their first meeting in June 1837 through the unhappy day in May 1839 when a decline in the Whigs' power forced Melbourne's government to resign.

### June 24, 1837
At 11 came Lord Melbourne and stayed till 12. He is a very honest, good and kindhearted, as well as very clever man.

### June 28, 1838 [coronation day]
My excellent Lord Melbourne, who stood very close to me throughout the whole ceremony, was completely over- come at this moment [when she was crowned], and very much affected; he gave me such a kind, and I may say fatherly look.

### August 16, 1838 [after one of her first speeches to Parliament]
Spoke of my fear of reading it too low, or too loud, or too quick. "I thought you read it very well," he said kindly. I spoke of my great nervousness, which I said I feared I never would get over. "I won't flatter Your Majesty that you ever will; for I think people scarcely ever get over it; it belongs to a peculiar [special] temperament, sensitive and susceptible; that shyness gen- erally accompanies high and right feelings," said Lord Melbourne most kindly.

The British statesman William Lamb, better known by his aristo- cratic title, Lord Melbourne

### May 7, 1839
All all my happiness gone! That happy peaceful life destroyed, that dearest kind Lord Melbourne no more my minister. . . . At 10 m[inutes] past 12 came Lord Melbourne. . . . It was some minutes before I could muster up courage to go in—and when I did, I really thought my heart would break; he was standing near the window; I took that kind, dear hand of his, and sobbed and grasped his hand in both mine and looked at him and sobbed out, "You will not forsake me"; . . . and he gave me such a look of kindness, pity, and affection, and could hardly utter for tears, "Oh! No," in such a touching voice.

During the later years of Victoria's reign, two extraordinary prime ministers dominated the political scene: William Gladstone and Benjamin Disraeli. In many ways the men were opposites. Gladstone was a wealthy landed gentleman and a devout Christian who had graduated from some of the best schools in England. Disraeli, whose education was far less distinguished, was the first British prime minister of Jewish heritage, as well as the author of several romantic novels.

Victoria found Gladstone unbearably dull and awkward. She once complained that he addressed her as though she were a public meeting. Meanwhile, she adored Disraeli's witty political briefings and high-flown flattery. In a letter to her daughter Vicky, the queen described the prime minister as "full of poetry, romance and chivalry." For his part, Disraeli observed that "everyone likes flattery, and when you come to royalty you should lay it on with a trowel."

Victoria called William Gladstone a "mischievous firebrand, arrogant, tyrannical and obstinate."

For more than three decades, Gladstone and Disraeli battled it out in Parliament: first as rival cabinet members, then as rival leaders of the opposition party, and finally as prime ministers. Gladstone was a moderate Liberal who pushed through a number of reforms, including bills extending the vote and introducing the secret ballot. He promoted an ethical foreign policy that sometimes meant compromising Britain's interests in the name of fairness and morality. Disraeli, as leader of the Conservative Party, favored measures aimed at strengthening and extending the British Empire. Under his leadership Britain fought against Russian expansion and gained control of a new and important route to India, the Suez Canal.

Most importantly, Disraeli persuaded the queen to emerge from the long state of isolation that had followed the death of her beloved Albert. Under the spell of the prime minister's lively political reports and flattering comments, Victoria began to regain her enthusiasm for the business of government. In 1874 she presided over the ceremonial opening of Parliament for the first time in years. Other official public acts and appearances followed. Along with her return to the public eye came a resurgence of her popularity. To her subjects, the aging queen was more than the "mother of her people." She was becoming a national institution, a symbol of the strength, dignity, and stability of the British Empire.

Benjamin Disraeli won the queen's affection with his elaborate compliments and gossipy briefings.

## THE ROYAL HOUSEHOLD

Along with the prime minister, a number of other politicians were frequent visitors to the royal court. Chief among these were the members of the cabinet, who kept the queen informed on business in the various government departments. One of the most important cabinet ministers was the foreign secretary, responsible for relations with other countries and Britain's overseas possessions.

Victoria's first foreign secretary was her most troublesome. At the start of her reign, Lord Palmerston instructed the young queen in international relations, including the proper way to deal with foreign heads of state and ambassadors. At first, Victoria found his lessons informative and enjoyable. Over time, though, her attitude toward Palmerston changed. The headstrong minister often sent out foreign dispatches before she had a chance to review them or, even worse, ignored the changes she made. By 1850, the indignant queen was threatening to dismiss Palmerston if he continued his willful ways. She was delighted when he was forced to resign. She was less pleased a few years later when the popular politician began the first of two terms as prime minister.

Hundreds of other men served at the royal court, helping the queen in her daily life. The most important members of the royal household were drawn from the aristocracy. The lord chamberlain's tasks included arranging state visits and other major events. The lord steward managed household expenses and salaries, which were paid out of the queen's income. The master of the household supervised the servants and staff. Among the other major officeholders were the master of ceremonies, the captain of the bodyguard of gentlemen-at-arms, her majesty's treasurer, the lords-in-waiting, the master of the horse, and the master of the buckhounds. There was also a large medical team, comprised of physicians, surgeons, a dentist, a chemist, and a druggist.

After Prince Albert's death, a new office was added to the royal household: private secretary to the queen. The most memorable man to serve in that post was Sir Henry Ponsonby. For twenty-five years, this clever gentleman arranged the queen's schedule, sorted her papers, drafted her letters and speeches, and smoothed her contacts with government officials. Ponsonby's most valuable talent was knowing just how far to go in trying to persuade the queen to act against her own wishes. Sometimes a tactful hint was enough to sway her. At other times it was wiser to simply give way. "When she says that 2 and 2 make 5," the even-tempered secretary explained, "I say that I cannot help thinking they make 4. She replies there may be some truth in what I say, but she knows they make 5. Thereupon I drop the discussion. It is of no consequence and I leave it there."

## BEHIND THE SCENES

A small army of servants took care of the royal family and maintained the queen's residences. The male servants included footmen, groomsmen, gardeners, florists, cooks, stewards, butlers, waiters, kitchen boys, pages, drivers, porters, fire lighters, and chimney sweeps. Many of these men and boys worked long hours, often continuing their chores after the rest of the court had gone to bed. In return, the servants in the royal household earned better pay and benefits than those in most aristocratic homes. In addition to their salaries, they received free meals, lodging, and medical treatment. Victoria always insisted that all the household servants be treated with respect and kindness, and she thought of her personal servants as "belonging to her family."

Victoria's devoted private secretary, Henry Ponsonby

John Brown, pictured in his Highland hat, was the queen's faithful servant for more than thirty years.

Many people were critical of the queen's fondness for one particular servant, John Brown. This rugged, good-looking, self-confident Highlander had worked as a guide for Victoria and Albert in Scotland. After Albert's death the grieving queen came to regard Brown as her special friend and protector. Visitors to the royal court were scandalized by the casual way the man addressed his "betters." From time to time, Brown quarreled with the queen's grown children, the aristocratic members of the household, and visiting ministers. He once interrupted Prime Minister Gladstone with a stern "Ye've said enough." On another occasion, visitors were shocked to hear him exclaim, while trying to pin a cloak around the queen's shoulders, "Hoots, wumman, canna ye hold yer head still!"

To Victoria, though, the outspoken Highlander was a loyal companion whose blunt, honest, natural manners put her at ease. When he died in 1883, she was "crushed by the violence of this unexpected blow." The queen had a life-size statue erected in John Brown's honor at Balmoral, inscribed with a heartfelt tribute:

Friend more than servant, loyal, truthful, brave!
Self less than duty, even to the grave!

Queen Victoria's
mother, Victoria
Mary Louisa,
Duchess of Kent

# FOUR

# THE WOMEN
## of
# THE COURT

Even in the midst of regal state and formality
[Victoria is] alive to the kindly feelings of our nature.
She does not because she is a Queen forget that she is a woman.
~ THE OBSERVER (JULY 7, 1838)

QUEEN VICTORIA WAS A LIVING CONTRADICTION:
a strong female ruler in a society dominated by men. In some ways
her gender actually enhanced her position. Her subjects were
delighted to welcome a young woman to the throne after the unpop-
ular old kings who had preceded her. Her ministers were reluctant
to argue with her, because that went against their notion of the
proper way for a gentleman to treat a lady. A year after Victoria
became queen, the British newspaper the *Observer* explained her
widespread appeal this way: "Her sex awoke the gallantry—her manners, her disposition as manifested in her behavior, have won the
affection—of her subjects."

# EARLY INFLUENCES

The two earliest influences in Victoria's life were women. Her father died before her first birthday, leaving her to be raised by her mother, Victoria Mary Louisa, Duchess of Kent. The other constant companion of her youth was her governess, Baroness Louise Lehzen.

The Duchess of Kent was a possessive, domineering mother. Born and raised in Germany, she did not get along with her late husband's English relatives. With the help of Sir John Conroy, the ambitious manager of her household, she devised a system for separating her daughter from the rest of the royal family. Under the "Kensington system," the princess was brought up in virtual isolation at London's Kensington Palace. She slept in her mother's room. She had few playmates or visitors, and she was never permitted to speak with an outsider without a guardian present. The goal was to make Victoria completely dependent on her mother and Conroy, so that they would be the real power behind the throne if and when she became queen.

Baroness Louise Lehzen was young Victoria's governess and closest friend.

There was a flaw in the Kensington system, however. It did not take into account Victoria's natural spirit and determination. The princess loved her mother but did not trust her. As for Conroy, she came to detest him. The older she grew, the more she resented the endless attempts to control her. In her struggles against domination, she had one important ally, her devoted governess. Louise Lehzen gave the lonely girl the unconditional warmth and devotion she longed for. The baroness also encouraged Victoria to question her mother and Conroy's motives and to preserve her independence.

On the day she became queen, Victoria demonstrated the strength of both her feelings and her character. She banished Sir John Conroy from court forever.

She insisted on meeting with her ministers alone, and afterward she had her bed removed from her mother's chamber. The duchess would accompany her daughter to Buckingham Palace, but she would be lodged in a suite as far away from the queen as possible. She complained so long and loud about her loss of status that Victoria came to view her as "an enemy in the house." The queen and her mother would not patch up their differences until several years later, after Conroy finally retired and left England.

John Conroy's dreams of power ended when the young queen banished him from court.

The young monarch's treatment of her former governess could not have been more different. Lehzen was assigned a room next door to Victoria's at Buckingham Palace. She was appointed "lady attendant on the queen," a position that gave her wide-ranging influence over the royal household, as well as her mistress's personal life and correspondence. An entry in Victoria's journal, penned at the end of her first day as queen, reflected her satisfaction with the new arrangements: "Went down and said good-night to Mamma etc. My dear Lehzen will always remain with me."

## LADIES AND SCANDALS

Queen Victoria was constantly surrounded by men: government ministers, the gentlemen of the royal household, male servants and staff. The members of the household with whom she came into the closest contact, however, were women. Her ladies-in-waiting, who generally included eight "ladies of the bedchamber" and eight "women of the bedchamber," were the wives and widows of high-ranking aristocrats. These highborn women performed services such as attending the queen on ceremonial occasions and helping to entertain her guests and answer her correspondence. In addition, several unmarried daughters of aristocrats served as maids of honor. These accomplished young women entertained the queen by reading aloud or playing the piano, accompanied her on carriage drives and horseback rides, and conversed charmingly with her dinner guests. All the ladies of the court served in rotating schedules, a few weeks at a time, several times a year. The highest-ranking lady, the mistress of the robes, arranged their schedules and assisted in their training.

Being chosen to attend the queen was a great honor. It could also be deadly dull. The ladies of the court were not allowed to leave the residence except when accompanying their royal mistress. They spent most of their time in a sitting room, awaiting Victoria's summons. During outings, all but the most favored ladies were expected to walk behind the queen, speaking only when spoken to and *never* interrupting.

Two controversial incidents involving the women of the royal household cast a shadow over the early months of Victoria's reign. The first episode centered on Lady Flora Hastings, a lady-in-waiting to the Duchess of Kent. The queen regarded "that odious Lady Flora" as a spy for her mother and John Conroy. When Flora's stomach began to swell, Victoria jumped to the conclusion that the unmarried woman was pregnant with Conroy's child. Vicious rumors spread through the court and the aristocracy, ending only after doctors determined that Flora actually had cancer. Victoria made her apologies shortly before the unfortunate woman's death, but her role in the scandal put an end to her early popularity. The crowds that had cheered when she first took the throne now hissed and threw stones at her carriage.

A second crisis came fast on the heels of this scandal. In May 1839 Prime Minister Melbourne was forced to resign when the Whigs began to lose support in Parliament. Victoria despised the incoming Tory prime minister, Sir Robert Peel. When Peel asked her to replace some of her Whig ladies with Tories, she flat-out refused. Peel's party did not have an overall majority in the House of Commons, and without the support of the crown, he determined that he could not form an effective government. He withdrew, and Melbourne remained in office for another two years. Critics including the English diarist Charles Greville were appalled that "the most momentous matters of Government and legislation" had been overturned by "the caprice of a young girl of nineteen." Meanwhile, many of Victoria's subjects applauded her determination. When the queen drove to church on the Sunday following the incident, crowds greeted her with cries of "Bravo!" and "The Queen for ever!"

## CLEANING HOUSE

In 1841 Victoria once again faced the prospect of Robert Peel as prime minister. This time the change of governments went smoothly. The queen even agreed to appoint several Tory ladies-in-waiting. The reason behind her remarkable about-face was Prince Albert. Now that the queen was happily married, she was less distressed over losing Lord Melbourne. Under her husband's steadying influence, she was also learning to put the monarchy above politics.

Not all was peace and happiness in the royal household, however. From the beginning of Victoria's marriage, Albert and Louise Lehzen had taken a strong dislike to each other. The former governess viewed the prince as a threat to her authority and never missed a chance to point out his shortcomings. For his part, Albert quickly realized that he would never be "master in my house" as long as Lehzen continued to serve as his wife's secretary and superintendent of the household.

After a few months of quiet fuming, the prince made a stand: his wife must choose between her meddlesome governess and her husband. Victoria argued and wept. At last, she gave in, and Baroness Lehzen was retired with a generous pension.

With Lehzen's departure, Albert was free to undertake a long-overdue review of the royal household. He found that two-thirds of the staff were completely unsupervised, resulting in inefficiency, waste, and confusion. The servants decided on their own when to start and stop work. They helped themselves to vast quantities of food, wine, candles, and other supplies. Rooms were often cold, because the servants in one household department were in charge of laying fires, while those in a second department lit them. Windows were seldom clean, because different departments were responsible for washing the insides and the outsides. Albert's chief adviser, Baron Christian Stockmar, illustrated the nonsensical system by describing the procedures for repairing a broken window in a kitchen cupboard:

> A requisition is prepared and signed by the Chief Cook, it is then countersigned by the Clerk of the Kitchen, then it is taken to be signed by the Master of the Household, thence it is taken to the Lord Chamberlain's Office, where it is authorized, and then laid before the Clerk of the Works . . . and consequently many a window and cupboard have remained broken for months.

With Stockmar's help, Albert set to work reorganizing the household. He dismissed the most corrupt and incompetent servants and put one official in charge of coordinating the work of those remaining. He introduced strict measures for eliminating waste and corruption. Newspaper articles and cartoons portrayed the prince as a petty taskmaster obsessed with counting scrub brushes and candle ends. However, Albert's efforts turned the royal household into a model of efficiency. His economies also saved enough money for the royal couple to buy Osborne House and Balmoral Castle entirely out of the queen's income.

# THE "WICKED FOLLY" OF FEMINISM

In the mid-nineteenth century, a growing number of women began to push for greater educational, professional, and legal rights. The presence of a strong woman on the British throne was a great inspiration to these early feminists. The queen herself, however, strongly opposed the developing women's rights movement. Like most Victorians, she believed that a woman's place was in the home, not in the rough-and-tumble worlds of business and politics (except in her own special case, of course). In 1870, after learning that an acquaintance named Lady Amberley had given a speech at a women's suffrage (voting rights) meeting, Victoria dashed off this outraged letter:

> The Queen is most anxious to enlist everyone who can speak or write to join in checking this mad, wicked folly of "Woman's Rights," with all its attendant horrors, on which her poor feeble sex is bent [resolved], forgetting every sense of womanly feeling and propriety. Lady Amberley ought to get a *good whipping.* It is a subject which makes the Queen so furious that she cannot contain herself. God created men and women different—then let them remain each in their own position. . . . Woman would become the most hateful, heartless, and disgusting of human beings were she allowed to unsex herself; and where would be the protection which man was intended to give the weaker sex?

*Above*: Early feminists advertise the latest issue of the suffragette journal *Votes for Women*.

Victoria with her oldest son
and heir, Albert Edward,
Prince of Wales

# FIVE

# FAMILY LIFE

Mid pleasures and palaces though we may roam,
Be it ever so humble, there's no place like home.
∾ "Home, Sweet Home" (Victorian-era poem and song)

THE FAMILY WAS THE CENTER OF VICTORIAN LIFE.
Amid the social upheavals of the Industrial Revolution, the Victorians turned to the home as a peaceful haven from the pressures and temptations of the modern world. One prominent English clergyman urged wives to "make a home something like a bright, serene, restful, joyful nook of heaven in an unheavenly world."

The Victorians' reverence for the home was matched by an intense interest in the family life of their queen. Past monarchs had been distant figures. Now the growth of newspapers and the new art of photography brought the queen right into her subjects' homes. People were fascinated by images of the royal family posing amid the splendors of Windsor Castle or relaxing at Osborne House. They applauded the royal couple's devotion to each other and affection for their children. To the middle class especially, Victoria, Albert, and their offspring became a model of the ideal family life.

## NINE LITTLE ROYALS

Victoria and Albert had a large family. Their first child, Princess Victoria ("Vicky"), was born nine months after their marriage. Eight more children followed over the next sixteen years: Albert Edward (nicknamed "Bertie"), Alice, Alfred ("Affie"), Helena ("Lenchen"), Louise, Arthur, Leopold, and Beatrice ("Baby").

The constant additions to the royal nursery were especially remarkable considering the fact that Victoria loathed childbearing and was not overly fond of babies. In the queen's opinion, women who were "always *enceinte* [pregnant]" were "quite disgusting; it is more like a rabbit or guinea-pig than anything else and really it is not very nice." Childbirth was not only painful but also "a complete violence to all one's feelings of propriety." While she loved children, she thought that "very young ones" were "rather disgusting." She could feel nothing for them "till they have become a little human; an ugly baby is a very nasty object—and the prettiest is frightful when undressed."

The size of the royal family was also noteworthy in light of the state of health care in the nineteenth century. Even among the wealthy, childbirth was hazardous to both mother and baby, and many infants died from infections and other causes. Victoria helped make childbearing a little easier for her female subjects when she allowed her doctors to use chloroform, an experimental anesthetic (painkiller), during the delivery of her last two babies. Members of the clergy protested that God intended for women to give birth in pain. Victoria dismissed their absurd arguments, and many women (at least those who could afford it) soon followed her lead.

There was one area of motherhood in which the queen was not so fortunate. She was an unknowing carrier of the hereditary disorder hemophilia. This rare condition, which can cause uncontrolled bleeding, is passed on by women but occurs only in men. Victoria and Albert's eighth child, Leopold, died at age thirty-one as a result of hemophilia. Two of their daughters, Alice and Beatrice, became carriers. Through their marriages the "royal disease" would eventually spread to many of the crown families of Europe.

Prince Leopold, the youngest of Victoria and Albert's sons, suffered from the "royal disease" of hemophilia.

## SCHOOL DAYS, PLAY DAYS

In most well-to-do Victorian households, children lived separate lives from their fond but distant parents: first in the nursery, where they were raised by nursemaids and governesses, and later at boarding schools. By those standards, the royal family was exceptionally close. Prince Albert spent a great deal of time in the nursery, playing with the children and overseeing their care. The queen, too, enjoyed her growing family. While her husband would always remain first in her affections, she found "true happiness" in the "domestic circle." When she took her "chicks" for a walk or watched them romping with their father, she was sure that "no Royal Ménage is to be found equal to ours."

Victoria and Albert also kept a close eye on their children's education. The little princes and princesses studied six days a week, under a succession of governesses and tutors. Their lessons included French, German, history, politics, geography, math, science, religion, art, and music. To ensure that they would not grow up too proud, they were fed a simple diet (boiled beef and milk pudding were staples on the dull menu) and often dressed in hand-me-down clothes. At the same time, their playmates were chosen with care, to avoid any "impure" influences. Albert himself selected a few wellborn boys to play with Bertie, then kept watch just in case "they should throw bread pellets at each other or talk lewdly."

Some of the royal children thrived under their careful upbringing. Vicky proved to be an exceptionally bright girl, speaking French and German by age three. Louise became a talented artist, and Affie taught himself the violin. Bertie, however, was a constant disappointment. As the firstborn son and heir to the throne, he was assigned the most demanding course of study. Unfortunately, the good-natured boy was no scholar. No matter how often his parents scolded him or tinkered with his schedule, he continued to care more about clothes and hunting than learning.

Even for Bertie, life was not all lessons. There were also family plays, musical assemblies, birthday parties, and vacations. Best of all were the times the family spent at Osborne House. In this homey residence, the royal couple and their offspring ate, walked, rode, and painted together. Albert flew kites and blew up balloons. He set aside dignity to teach his oldest son how to do somersaults. He even built a full-size wooden cottage for the children. This delightful building—part playhouse, part schoolhouse—was modeled on a real Swiss chalet. There was a fully equipped kitchen for the girls and a carpenter shop for the boys. A miniature natural history museum held an ever-growing collection of shells, stones, fossils, and other curiosities. Outside there were nine garden plots, where each child could grow flowers and vegetables with his or her own set of tools. The Swiss Cottage became the royal children's favorite place on earth, and it would remain one of the fondest memories of their childhood.

The purpose of the royal children's education, of course, was to prepare them for their future roles in life. Edward would one day succeed his mother on the throne. The younger boys were trained for high positions in the army and navy. The daughters, like nearly all young Victorian women, were expected to marry.

Victoria was pregnant with her last child when she began planning the wedding of her first. Princess Victoria was just seventeen when she married Prince Frederick William of Prussia, who would later become emperor of Germany. Seven of the remaining eight royal sons and daughters also married into European royal families. (Louise married the Marquis of Lorne, a future governor-general of Canada.) Through Victoria's children and grandchildren, Britain was linked with the reigning families of countries including Germany, France, Italy, Spain, Greece, Norway, Sweden, Denmark, Romania, and Russia. The queen's far-flung connections earned her the affectionate title "grandmother of Europe."

# THE QUEEN IS AMUSED

Queen Victoria is often portrayed as a somber old woman. One well-known story recalls the time she responded to a slightly improper joke with a frosty "We are not amused." Kaiser Wilhelm II of Germany, the son of Queen Victoria's oldest daughter, liked to tell another story that showed his grandmother was not as humorless as many people thought.

In 1878 the queen had invited an elderly naval officer to join her for lunch. For a while the two discussed the recent sinking of a naval training ship, the *Eurydice*. Then Victoria changed the subject, inquiring after the admiral's sister. "Well, Ma'am," shouted the nearly deaf seaman, "I'm going to have her turned over and take a good look at her bottom and have it well scraped." There was a moment of stunned silence. Then, wrote the kaiser, "My grandmother put down her knife and fork, hid her face in her handkerchief and shook and heaved with laughter until the tears rolled down her face."

Victoria's relations with her grown children could be difficult. While she wrote to them constantly, her letters were as likely to contain rebukes as endearments. "Far or near . . . my love and affection and solicitude [care] will ever be the same, my beloved Child," she wrote on Vicky's twentieth birthday. In less sentimental letters, she criticized her daughter's writing style and temperament and warned her that "as a rule children are a bitter disappointment."

As for Bertie, Victoria continued to fret that her oldest son was too idle and lazy to ever take the throne. At the same time, she doted on "poor, foolish Bertie," as she did all her children. The future king of England was over thirty years old and the father of five children when he took a trip to India. One can only imagine how he felt when a runner appeared in his remote jungle camp, bearing a telegram from his mother reminding him to get to bed by ten o'clock.

Following Albert's death, Victoria insisted that one of her daughters remain with her at all times. That role eventually fell to the youngest girl, Beatrice. After all her sisters had married and left home, "Baby" stayed with her mother as a companion and helpmate. Everyone expected the shy, lonely princess to remain an "old maid" for life. Then, at age twenty-seven, Beatrice fell in love with a handsome German prince, Henry of Battenberg. Victoria was furious. For six months she refused to speak to her daughter. Finally, she agreed to the marriage, on the condition that the couple would always live under her roof. In time the queen came to regard her charming son-in-law as "the sunbeam in our Home." And when grandchildren began to fill the nursery, she found new joy in the sound of "the little feet & merry voices above."

# REMEMBERING GRANDMAMMA

Queen Victoria had forty grandchildren. To the little royals who knew her best, she was a doting grandmother who laughed at their antics, took them for rides in her carriage, and spoiled them with presents. To the grandchildren who lived farther away, however, the regal monarch could sometimes be an intimidating figure. Princess Marie, the daughter of the queen's second son, Alfred, described one childhood visit to "Grandmamma."

The hush round Grandmamma's door was awe-inspiring, it was like approaching the mystery of some sanctuary.

Silent, soft-carpeted corridors led to Grandmamma's apartments which were somehow always approached from afar off, and those that led the way towards them, were they servant, lady or maid, talked in hushed voices and trod softly as though with felt soles.

One door after another opened noiselessly, it was like passing through the forecourts of a temple, before approaching the final mystery to which only the initiated had access.

Wonderful little old Grandmamma, who, though such a small, unimposing little woman to look at, should have known so extraordinarily how to inspire reverential fear! Our nurses would drive us along before them like a troop of well-behaved little geese, they too having suddenly become soft-tongued and even their scoldings were as words breathed through a flannel so that all sharpness was taken out of their voices of reproof.

When finally the door was opened, there sat Grandmamma not idol-like at all, not a bit frightening, smiling a kind little smile, almost as shy as us children.

*Above*: "Grandmamma" in her later years, with two of her twenty-two granddaughters

Lords and ladies dine in splendor at a Victorian formal dinner party.

# SIX

# GOLDEN DAYS and TROUBLED TIMES

It was only yesterday; but what a gulf between now and then!

⁓ WILLIAM MAKEPEACE THACKERAY (1860)

QUEEN VICTORIA WORKED HARD, BUT SHE ALSO KNEW how to play. In the early years of her reign especially, the royal court was the site of many splendid entertainments. There were formal dinners, with dozens of richly prepared dishes. There were dazzling dances, where finely dressed lords and ladies waltzed to the music of the court orchestra. The queen also indulged her love of music with private concerts by famous opera companies, choral groups, and solo singers and musicians.

In later years much of the queen's leisure time revolved around her family. She spent her favorite days hiking, riding, and relaxing with Albert and the children at Osborne House and Balmoral Castle.

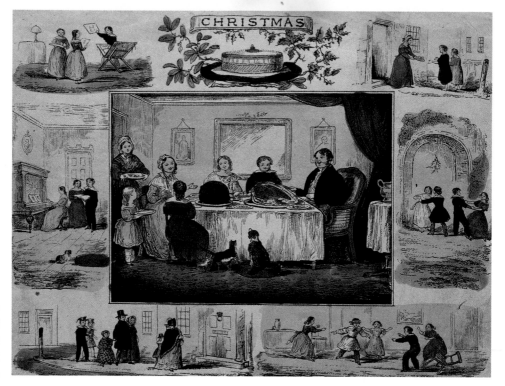

Scenes of holiday cheer decorate one of the first Christmas cards, created in the early 1840s.

Family birthdays were celebrated with music, poetry reading, flowers, and gifts. Christmas was a time for feasting, caroling, and presents for the entire household. In 1841 Albert set up the first Christmas tree at Windsor Castle, importing a German tradition that was soon copied all over England. A lord-in-waiting described one "jolly Christmas day" at Windsor, where more than a dozen trees sparkled with "bonbons and coloured wax lights. . . . Even as in a public bazaar, where people jostle one another, so lords, grooms, Queen and princes laughed and talked [and] forgot to bow."

## CHEERS FOR THE YOUNG QUEEN

Most of Victoria's subjects never got a peek inside Windsor Castle or any of the other royal residences. They could still share in some of the major events of their queen's life, however, through public celebrations. The first of these lavish spectacles was the coronation.

Victoria was formally crowned on June 28, 1838, about a year after she ascended the throne. The event was carefully designed to inspire enthusiasm and loyalty among her subjects. Half a million noisy, jostling people lined the roundabout route from Buckingham Palace to Westminster Abbey. They raised thunderous cheers for the procession of marching bands, soldiers, and cavalrymen, followed by the youthful queen riding in an ornate carriage pulled by eight cream-colored horses. After the long coronation ceremony, Victoria returned to the palace. She promptly took off her finery and gave her pet dog, Dash, a bath. Meanwhile, the crowds in London enjoyed fireworks, a fair, and free entry to theaters and other places of entertainment.

The next major event in the young queen's life was her wedding, in February 1840. The bride wore a white satin gown and a wreath of orange flower blossoms. The groom looked pale but handsome in a British military uniform. (Parliament had just passed an act making him a British subject.) Victoria was "quite touched" by the "immense crowd of people" who shouted congratulations to the happy couple all the way from Buckingham Palace to Windsor Castle, where they spent their honeymoon.

## THE GREAT EXHIBITION

Prince Albert had a vision of a world in which all peoples would live together in peace, bound together not by force of arms but by the free interchange of goods and ideas. In early 1850 he began work on a project to further that goal. The Great Exhibition would showcase Britain's tremendous advances in science, industry, and technology. At the same time, all nations would be invited to display their finest products at what would become the first world's fair.

The Great Exhibition opened in London's Hyde Park on May 1, 1851. It was housed inside a gigantic glass hall that was longer than

five football fields and tall enough to enclose the park's giant elms. Inside this "Crystal Palace" were some 14,000 displays from all over the world. Visitors admired beautiful Persian carpets, Indian silks, Chinese lanterns, Spanish mantillas, Swiss clocks, and German porcelain. They gaped at exotic stuffed animals, a Tunisian lion-skin tent, and an entire Turkish bazaar. They shook their heads over oddities including a collapsible piano, a garden seat carved from coal, and an alarm bed that dumped its lazy occupant into a tub of water. Most impressive of all were the displays of invention and technology: enormous steam engines, high-speed printing presses, textile machines, an electric telegraph. While many of the industrial triumphs were British, there were also American inventions, including the McCormick mechanical reaper, the Singer sewing machine, and the Colt revolver.

The Great Exhibition was a spectacular success. By the time it closed in October, more than 6 million people from all over the country and the world had come to marvel at its wonders. The queen herself visited at least forty times. She was fascinated by the "ingenious" inventions and delighted to meet "so many clever people I should never have known otherwise." Most of all, she was thrilled by the praise heaped upon her beloved husband. "Albert's dearest name is immortalised with this great conception," she wrote proudly, "and my own dear country showed she was worthy of it."

## THE QUEEN'S JUBILEES

In 1887 Britain celebrated the queen's Golden Jubilee—the fiftieth anniversary of her ascension to the throne. All over the empire, prisoners were set free in her honor. Hospital patients in Singapore enjoyed extra rations of rice. Buddhist monks in Burma (modern-day Myanmar) received special Jubilee robes. Towns and villages throughout England held festive dinners, parades, and fireworks. On June 21, set aside as a national day of thanksgiving, Victoria rode through London in an open carriage. One lady-in-waiting was awed by the "millions of people thronging the streets like an anthill. . . . It was one continuous roar of cheering from the moment she came out of the door of her Palace till the instant she got back to it! Deafening."

As splendid as the Golden Jubilee was, nothing could compare to the pageantry of 1897. The Diamond Jubilee would pay tribute to Victoria's sixty years on the throne—a longer reign than any other British monarch. It would also celebrate a far-flung empire at the height of its pride, wealth, and power.

On the morning of June 22, hordes of people packed London's sidewalks, balconies, and rooftops for the grandest procession the city had ever seen. First came the leaders of Britain's dominions and colonies, flanked by their honor guards: Australian lancers with plumed helmets, scarlet-clad Canadian Mounties, turbaned Sikhs from India, camelback regiments from New Borneo, police from Hong Kong in colorful robes and cone-shaped hats. Next came a colorful succession of British troops, some marching in formation, others on horseback. Following the military parade was a long line of carriages bearing princes and princesses from all across Europe.

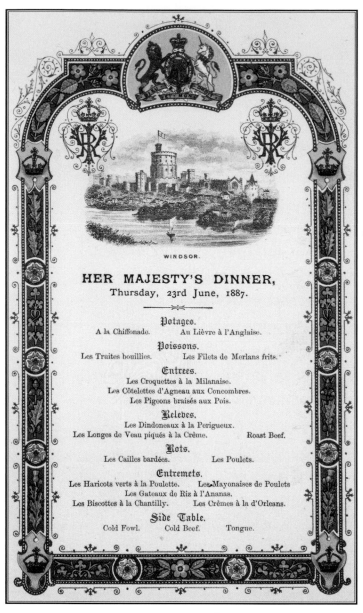

WINDSOR.

**HER MAJESTY'S DINNER,**
Thursday, 23rd June, 1887.

Potages.
A la Chiffonade.          Au Lièvre à l'Anglaise.

Poissons.
Les Truites bouillies.          Les Filets de Merlans frits.

Entrees.
Les Croquettes à la Milanaise.
Les Côtelettes d'Agneau aux Concombres.
Les Pigeons braisés aux Pois.

Releves.
Les Dindoneaux à la Perigueux.
Les Longes de Veau piqués à la Crème.          Roast Beef.

Rots.
Les Cailles bardées.          Les Poulets.

Entremets.
Les Haricots verts à la Poulette.     Les Mayonaises de Poulets
Les Gateaux de Riz à l'Ananas.
Les Biscottes à la Chantilly.          Les Crèmes à la d'Orleans.

Side Table.
Cold Fowl.          Cold Beef.          Tongue.

The menu from a royal dinner served up during the queen's Golden Jubilee

Last of all came the queen's carriage, drawn by eight horses draped in gold and scarlet. "No one ever, I believe, has met with such an ovation as was given to me," Victoria later wrote in her journal. "The crowds were quite indescribable, and their enthusiasm truly marvelous and deeply touching." Close observers saw tears trickling down the queen's cheeks during the six-mile procession.

The Diamond Jubilee celebrations continued for two more weeks. Victoria attended services, receptions, dinners, garden parties, and a naval show. She reviewed British and colonial troops, fire brigades, and schoolboys, all pledging their devotion to their monarch. When it was all over, she issued an open letter to her people, which was published in the *Times* of London:

It is difficult for me on this occasion to say how truly touched and grateful I am for the spontaneous and universal outburst of loyal attachment and real affection which I have experienced on the completion of the sixtieth year of my reign. . . . It has given me unbounded pleasure to see so many of my subjects from all parts of the world assembled here . . . , and I would wish to thank them all from the depth of my grateful heart.

## THE YEAR OF REVOLUTIONS

Public spectacles like the Great Exhibition and the Queen's Jubilees reflected a nation proud of its power, progress, and prosperity. But everything was not always rosy in Victorian times. The early years of Victoria's reign were marked by social and political unrest. The turmoil was brought on largely by the rapid changes that came with industrialization, which led to problems including poverty and hunger.

Conditions were especially grim in the 1840s, when an economic depression and poor harvests left many people without enough to eat. Nowhere was the suffering of the "Hungry Forties" greater than in Ireland. From 1845 to 1850, a fungus known as "potato blight" destroyed the potato crop, the country's main source of food and income. The British government provided some relief, but not enough to avert a terrible famine. More than a million Irish men, women, and children died of starvation and disease. Hundreds of thousands emigrated, settling in countries including England, Scotland, Canada, and the United States. The Great Irish Famine was the worst catastrophe of Victoria's reign, and it would poison relations between England and Ireland for generations to come.

In England the turmoil of the Hungry Forties erupted in frequent protests, sometimes peaceful, sometimes violent. Many middle- and upper-class Britons feared that the lower classes would rise up in armed revolution. The anxiety reached its peak in 1848, when a wave of revolutions swept across Europe, threatening or overthrowing governments in France, Austria-Hungary, Italy, and Germany.

In March 1848 there were riots in several English towns and cities. A protest organization known as the Chartists announced

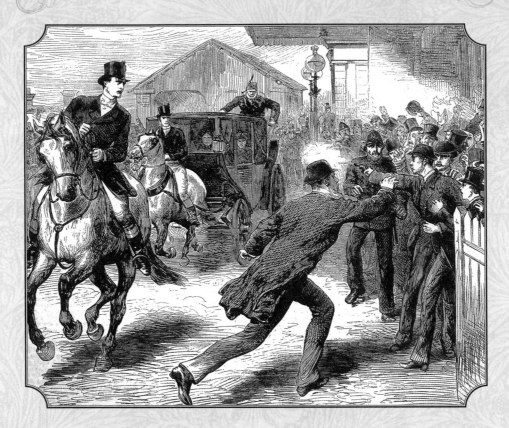

# WOULD-BE ASSASSINS

Despite her popularity, Queen Victoria faced seven assassination attempts during her long reign. The first came in June 1840, when a mentally ill man fired two shots at the carriage in which the newly married queen was riding with her husband. As passersby seized the assailant, Victoria and Albert calmly continued their drive.

Further assassination attempts took place in 1842 (twice), 1849, 1850, 1872, and 1882. In one attack the assailant whacked the queen over the head with a walking stick while she was out riding with her children. That night she attended the opera with a black eye and received a standing ovation.

In the last attempt on the queen's life, a deranged poet shot at her carriage. Two schoolboys pummeled the assailant with their umbrellas until the police arrived and disarmed him. Afterward Victoria received so many letters and telegrams from her loyal subjects that she declared it was "worth being shot at—to see how much one is loved."

*Above*: A young Scottish poet named Roderick Maclean takes a shot at Victoria's carriage in 1882.

plans for a huge march on London, where demonstrators would present a "People's Charter" demanding greater rights for working men. The British government stationed thousands of troops in the capital and stocked the Houses of Parliament with supplies for a long siege. On April 10 the Chartists' march fizzled out in a deluge of rain. The expected uprising never came.

Historians have many different views on how the English managed to escape the upheavals that engulfed so much of Europe. Some point to the Victorians' respect for order and tradition and their faith in their constitutional government. That faith would be rewarded in the decades to come, as Parliament passed laws that gradually improved the lot of working people. Victoria herself gave credit to "the loyalty of the people at large . . . and their indignation at their peace being interfered with by such wanton and worthless men."

## QUEEN VICTORIA'S WARS

From 1854 to 1856, the British joined with France and the Ottoman Empire (now Turkey) in a campaign to limit Russia's growing power in the Middle East. Much of the fighting took place on the Crimean Peninsula in the Black Sea. More than 100,000 British soldiers were sent to fight in the Crimean War. About 4,000 were killed in battle, often because of incompetent leadership. More than 16,000 died from disease. Through the new electric telegraph, the first "war correspondents" sent daily reports on the brutal battles and the appalling conditions in military hospitals. The British public raised such an outcry that the government sent the pioneering nurse Florence Nightingale to the Crimea. Nightingale's methods—based on revolutionary ideas about the importance of cleanliness in hospitals—sharply reduced the death toll, while laying the foundations for the modern nursing profession.

After the Crimean War, the British would not take part in any major European conflict until the beginning of World War I in 1914. However, this period of relative peace at home was also a time of rampant empire building. It was the age of imperialism, when European nations were competing for control of vast territories in Asia, Africa, and other parts of the world. Great Britain's superior navy gave it a huge advantage in this contest. At the same time, resistance from native forces embroiled Britain in a series of overseas conflicts that one historian has called "Queen Victoria's little wars."

One of the most violent of these foreign wars took place in India. The people of India had long objected to the East India Company's rule over much of the subcontinent. In May 1857 the simmering resentments erupted in a bloody rebellion by soldiers in the British-controlled Indian army. The violence quickly spread across northern India. Hundreds of British soldiers and civilians, including many women and children, were slaughtered. British troops responded with equally savage reprisals. When the fighting finally died down, the British government took direct control of India. Queen Victoria issued a proclamation promising "generosity, benevolence and religious toleration" to her new subjects. For the remainder of her reign—in fact, until the end of World War II some ninety years later—India would remain the "jewel in the crown" of the British Empire.

Britain's imperial ambitions also led to bloodshed across Africa. In 1879 the Zulus of southern Africa fought to defend their lands from British aggression. Armed only with spears and shields, Zulu warriors inflicted a series of crushing (and embarrassing) defeats on the invaders. Within a few months, however, the Zulus were subdued by the larger and better-equipped British forces.

Five years later, Britain faced an uprising in the Sudan, south of British-controlled Egypt. Rebel forces under a religious leader known as the Mahdi threatened to overrun the Sudanese capital of Khartoum. General Charles Gordon was sent to evacuate British and Egyptian residents. Soon after he arrived, the rebels surrounded the city. The entire British nation held its breath as a relief column made its way up the Nile River. The rescuers arrived two days too late. Khartoum had fallen after a 313-day siege, and all the defenders had been massacred.

The end of the century brought further conflicts in southern Africa. Gold and diamonds had been discovered in the Transvaal, an independent republic established by white African farmers of Dutch descent, known as the Boers. The British were determined to seize the rich region. They expected to overcome the inexperienced soldier-farmers quickly. Instead, the Boer War was long and costly, lasting three years and claiming more than 50,000 military and civilian casualties.

For Queen Victoria, there was never any question of giving up the fight for the Transvaal. The Boer War was "not only necessary, it was just," she maintained. It would be "fought to the end" so that the brave soldiers of the British army "should not be allowed to suffer in vain." In 1899 a government minister who brought the queen a gloomy war report was cut short with this regal pronouncement: "Please understand that there is no depression in *this* house; we are not interested in the possibilities of defeat; they do not exist."

## FINAL DAYS

Well into her final years, Queen Victoria continued to play an active role in government affairs and the doings of her ever-growing family. But as the year 1901 began, the effects of her eighty-two years were showing. Her eyesight was failing. She had become so lame that she had to be wheeled about in a chair. She had trouble sleeping at night

Queen Victoria at age seventy-eight, around the time of her Diamond Jubilee

and staying awake during the day, and she found it increasingly difficult to concentrate. On January 12 she made her last entry in the journal that she had started as a teenager. Ten days later, she died at Osborne House, surrounded by her children and grandchildren.

Newspapers all across the world carried the news of Queen Victoria's passing. Foreign heads of state sent words of sorrow and sympathy to the new king, Edward VII, and the rest of the royal family. Meanwhile, in the streets of London, people wandered about with sad, anxious faces. Many had lived their whole lives knowing only one monarch. The small, plump, unfailingly regal old woman had come to seem like a never-ending force of nature. She had embodied the virtues and achievements of her times, the progress and prosperity that the Victorians were so proud of. For her subjects, her death was more than the loss of a beloved monarch. It was the end of the Victorian Age, and the beginning of a whole new era.

# GLOSSARY

**constitutional monarchy** A form of government in which the head of state is a king or queen whose powers are restricted by the country's laws and constitution.

**dominions** Self-governing territories of the British Empire.

**hemophilia** A rare hereditary condition in which the blood does not clot, so that even a minor wound can result in uncontrolled bleeding. Queen Victoria was a carrier of hemophilia.

**imperialism** A policy in which a nation seeks to expand its power and influence by gaining control of other territories.

**Industrial Revolution** The historical period marking the introduction of power-driven machinery and the social changes that resulted. The Industrial Revolution began in England in the mid- to late 1700s.

**Parliament** The national legislature of Great Britain.

**Sikhs** Followers of a religion called Sikhism, which was founded in India in the late 1400s. In Victorian times Sikhs were an important part of the British Indian army.

**Tories** Members of a British political party that often supported policies favoring the landed aristocracy and the church and opposed reform efforts. The Tory Party eventually became known as the Conservative Party.

**Whigs** Members of a British political party that passed major reform bills in the mid-1800s. The Whig Party eventually became known as the Liberal Party.

## FOR FURTHER READING

Ashby, Ruth. *Victorian England.* New York: Marshall Cavendish, 2003.

Brocklehurst, Ruth. *Victorians.* London: Usborne Publishing, 2004.

Chiflet, Jean-Loup, and Alain Beaulet. *Victoria and Her Times.* New York: Henry Holt, 1996.

Damon, Duane C. *Life in Victorian England.* New York: Thomson Gale, 2006.

Mitchell, Sally. *Daily Life in Victorian England.* Westport, CT: Greenwood Press, 1996.

Price-Groff, Claire. *Queen Victoria and Nineteenth-Century England.* New York: Marshall Cavendish, 2003.

Swisher, Clarice, ed. *Victorian England.* San Diego, CA: Greenhaven Press, 2000.

Whitelaw, Nancy. *Queen Victoria and the British Empire.* Greensboro, NC: Morgan Reynolds, 2005.

## ONLINE INFORMATION

*Historic Figures: Victoria (1819-1901).* BBC.
   www.bbc.co.uk/history/historic_figures/victoria_queen.shtml
*Monarchs of Britain: Victoria (1837-1901 A.D.)* Brittania.
   www.britannia.com/history/monarchs/mon58.html
*Queen Victoria.* Spartacus Educational.
   www.spartacus.schoolnet.co.uk/PRvictoria.htm
*Queen Victoria's Empire.* PBS.
   www.pbs.org/empires/victoria/
*The Victorians: Queen Victoria.* Woodlands Junior School, Tonbridge, Kent, England.
   www.woodlands-junior.kent.sch.uk/Homework/victorians/victoria.htm
*Victorian Station: The Life and Times of Queen Victoria.*
   www.victorianstation.com/queen.html

## SELECTED BIBLIOGRAPHY

Arnstein, Walter L. *Queen Victoria.* New York: Palgrave Macmillan, 2003.

Auchincloss, Louis. *Persons of Consequence: Queen Victoria and Her Circle.* New York: Random House, 1979.

De-la-Noy, Michael. *Queen Victoria at Home.* New York: Carroll and Graf, 2003.

Ferguson, Niall. *Empire: The Rise and Demise of the British World Order and the Lessons for Global Power.* New York: Basic Books, 2002.

Hibbert, Christopher. *Queen Victoria: A Personal History.* New York: Basic Books, 2000.

King, Greg. *Twilight of Splendor: The Court of Queen Victoria during Her Diamond Jubilee Year.* Hoboken, NJ: John Wiley, 2007.

Lasdun, Susan. *Victorians at Home.* New York: Viking, 1981.

Longford, Elizabeth. *Queen Victoria: Born to Succeed.* New York: Harper and Row, 1964.

Mullen, Richard, and James Munson. *Victoria: Portrait of a Queen.* London: BBC Books, 1987.

Nash, Roy. *Buckingham Palace: The Place and the People.* London: Macdonald, 1980.

Nevill, Barry St-John, ed. *Life at the Court of Queen Victoria, 1861-1901.* Exeter, England: Webb and Bower, 1984.

Packard, Jerrold M. *Victoria's Daughters.* New York: St. Martin's, 1998.

St. Aubyn, Giles. *Queen Victoria: A Portrait.* New York: Atheneum, 1992.

Strachey, Lytton. *Queen Victoria.* New York: Harcourt, Brace, and World, 1921.

Thompson, Dorothy. *Queen Victoria: The Woman, the Monarchy, and the People.* New York: Pantheon, 1990.

Victoria, Queen. *Leaves from the Journal of Our Life in the Highlands from 1848-1861.* Edited by Arthur Helps. Leipzig, Germany: Bernard Tauchnitz, 1884.

———. *Queen Victoria in Her Letters and Journals.* Edited by Christopher Hibbert. New York: Viking, 1985.

York, Sarah Mountbatten-Windsor, Duchess of, with Benita Stoney. *Victoria and Albert: A Family Life at Osborne.* New York: Prentice Hall, 1991.

## SOURCES FOR QUOTATIONS

### ABOUT VICTORIAN ENGLAND

p. 6 "Since it has pleased": Victoria, *Letters and Journals*, p. 23.

p. 7 "an age of transition": Sir Henry Holland, "The Progress and Spirit of Physical Science," *Edinburgh Review*, July 1858, quoted at www.archive.org/stream/essaysonscientif00hollrich/ essaysonscientif00hollrich_djvu.txt

### CHAPTER 1: VICTORIA'S EMPIRE

p. 9 "We seem": Sir John Robert Seeley, "The Expansion of England," 1883, at http://web.viu.ca/davies/H479B.Imperialism.Nationalism/ Seeley.Br.Expansion.imperial.1883.htm

p. 10 "run mad with loyalty": Mullen and Munson, *Victoria*, pp. 24-25.

p. 10 "reigns but does not rule": Paul Barry Clarke and Joe Foweraker, eds., *Encyclopedia of Democratic Thought* (New York: Routledge, 2001), p. 99.

p. 11 "I get so many": Victoria, *Letters and Journals*, p. 24.

p. 13 "The use of the Queen": Walter Bagehot, *The English Constitution* (reprint, Ithaca, NY: Cornell University Press, 1966), pp. 82, 111.

p. 16 "Here we see": "Interview with Lawrence James" at www.pbs.org/empires/victoria/empire/james.html

p. 18 "All things bright": Valentine Cunningham, *The Victorians: An Anthology of Poetry and Poetics* (Oxford: Blackwell Publishing, 2000), pp. 440-441.

p. 20 "the lower classes": Mullen and Munson, *Victoria*, p. 95.

p. 21 "yield to none": Victoria, *Letters and Journals*, p. 279.

### CHAPTER 2: SPLENDID PALACES AND "COZY" RETREATS

p. 23 "At a quarter-past seven": Victoria, *Letters and Journals*, p. 146.

p. 24 "I really and truly": ibid., p. 25.

p. 25 "a little shy": Hibbert, *Queen Victoria*, p. 86.

p. 25 "I cannot help": Lasdun, *Victorians at Home*, p. 69.

p. 25 "very sorry indeed": Victoria, *Letters and Journals*, p. 27.

p. 26 "a disgrace": St. Aubyn, *Queen Victoria*, p. 184.

p. 27 "live with my beloved": Victoria, *Letters and Journals*, pp. 95-96.

p. 27 "imagine a prettier": ibid., p. 96.

p. 28 "perfect little Paradise": ibid., p. 97.

p. 28 "our very own": Lasdun, *Victorians at Home*, p. 70.

p. 28 "pretty little castle": Victoria, *Leaves from the Journal*, p. 95.

p. 28 "great taste": Victoria, *Letters and Journals*, p. 146.

p. 29 "seeing a single": St. Aubyn, *Queen Victoria*, p. 194.

p. 31 "delightful, successful expedition" and "Breakfasted at Balmoral": Victoria, *Leaves from the Journal*, pp. 177, 180-183, 187.


## CHAPTER 3: THE MEN OF THE COURT

p. 33 "Oh! to feel": Victoria, *Letters and Journals*, p. 57.

p. 34 "not yet quite": Hibbert, *Queen Victoria*, p. 103.

p. 34 "it was 10 to 1": Victoria, *Letters and Journals*, p. 53.

p. 34 "perfection in every way": ibid., p. 57.

p. 34 "beautiful blue eyes": ibid., p. 56.

p. 35 "could not exist": Queen Victoria, *The Letters of Queen Victoria*, vol. 2, edited by Arthur Christopher Benson (London: John Murray, 1908), p. 242.

p. 35 "feverish attack": Queen Victoria, *Dearest Child*, edited by Roger Fulford (New York: Holt, Rinehart and Winston, 1964), p. 372.

p. 35 "my entire self": St. Aubyn, *Queen Victoria*, p. 329.

p. 36 "He doubts education": Auchincloss, *Persons of Consequence*, p. 25.

p. 37 "At 11 came Lord Melbourne": Victoria, *Letters and Journals*, pp. 24, 34, 36-37, 45-46.

p. 38 "full of poetry": ibid., p. 203.

p. 38 "everyone likes flattery": St. Aubyn, *Queen Victoria*, p. 427.

p. 41 "When she says": Hibbert, *Queen Victoria*, p. 334.

p. 41 "belonging to her family": King, *Twilight of Splendor*, p. 118.

p. 42 "Ye've said enough": Hibbert, *Queen Victoria*, p. 325.

p. 42 "Hoots, wumman": St. Aubyn, *Queen Victoria*, p. 357.

p. 43 "crushed by the violence": Victoria, *Letters and Journals*, p. 281.

p. 43 "Friend more than servant": St. Aubyn, *Queen Victoria*, p. 424.


## CHAPTER 4: THE WOMEN OF THE COURT

p. 45 "Even in the midst": Swisher, *Victorian England*, p. 34.

p. 45 "Her sex awoke the gallantry": ibid.

p. 47 " an enemy": Victoria, *Letters and Journals*, p. 42.

p. 47 "Went down": ibid., p. 24.

p. 48 "that odious": St. Aubyn, *Queen Victoria*, p. 96.

p. 49 "the most momentous": Hibbert, *Queen Victoria*, p. 97.

p. 49 "Bravo!": St. Aubyn, *Queen Victoria*, p. 114.

p. 49 "master in my house": ibid., p. 168.

p. 50 "A requisition is prepared": ibid., p. 179.

p. 51 "The Queen is most anxious": Strachey, *Queen Victoria*, p. 409-410.

## CHAPTER 5: FAMILY LIFE

p. 53 "Mid pleasures and palaces": "Home, Sweet Home" by John Howard Payne, 1822, at www.bartleby.com/102/14.html

p. 53 "make a home": James Baldwin Brown, *Our Morals and Manners* (London: Hodder and Stoughton, 1872), pp. 38-39.

p. 54 "always *enceinte*": Victoria, *Letters and Journals*, p. 113.

p. 54 "a complete violence": St. Aubyn, *Queen Victoria*, p. 159.

p. 54 "very young ones" and "till they have": ibid., p. 167.

p. 55 "true happiness": ibid., p. 204.

p. 55 "no Royal Ménage": Queen Victoria, *The Letters of Queen Victoria*, vol. 1, edited by Arthur Christopher Benson (London: John Murray, 1908), p. 475.

p. 56 "they should throw": St. Aubyn, *Queen Victoria*, p. 203.

p. 57 "We are not amused": ibid., p. 498.

p. 57 "Well, Ma'am": Nevill, *Life at the Court of Queen Victoria*, p. 15.

p. 58 "Far or near": St. Aubyn, *Queen Victoria*, p. 264.

p. 58 "as a rule": Victoria, *Letters and Journals*, p. 241.

p. 58 "poor, foolish Bertie": ibid., p. 177.

p. 58 "the sunbeam": Queen Victoria, *Advice to My Grand-daughter*, edited by Richard Hough (New York: Simon and Schuster, 1975), p. 135.

p. 58 "the little feet": Longford, *Queen Victoria*, p. 569.

p. 59 "The hush round": Marie, Queen Consort of Ferdinand I, King of Romania, *The Story of My Life* (Manchester, NH: Ayer Publishing, 1971), p. 18.

## CHAPTER 6: GOLDEN DAYS AND TROUBLED TIMES

p. 61 "It was only yesterday": William Makepeace Thackeray, "De Jufentute," 1860, quoted in Walter E. Houghton, *The Victorian Frame of Mind* (New Haven, CT: Yale University Press, 1957), p. 3.

p. 62 "jolly Christmas day": Stanley Weintraub, *Uncrowned King: The Life of Prince Albert* (New York: Simon and Schuster, 1997), pp. 395-397.

p. 63 "quite touched": *Queen Victoria's Journal*, Royal Archives, quoted in Hibbert, *Queen Victoria*, p. 123.

p. 64 "ingenious" and "so many clever": Hibbert, *Queen Victoria*, p. 215.

p. 64 "Albert's dearest": Strachey, *Queen Victoria*, p. 202.

p. 65 "millions of people": St. Aubyn, *Queen Victoria*, p. 490.

p. 66 "No one ever": Victoria, *Letters and Journals*, p. 335.

p. 66 "It is difficult": King, *Twilight of Splendor*, p. 270-271.

p. 68 "worth being shot at": St. Aubyn, *Queen Victoria*, p. 421.

p. 69 "the loyalty of the people": ibid., p. 223.

p. 70 "Queen Victoria's little wars": Byron Farwell, *Queen Victoria's Little Wars* (New York: Harper and Row, 1985).

p. 70 "generosity, benevolence": Hibbert, *Queen Victoria*, p. 251.

p. 71 "not only necessary" and "Please understand": Mullen and Munson, *Victoria*, p. 140.

# INDEX

## ABOUT THE AUTHOR

**VIRGINIA SCHOMP** wrote her first short story (starring a magical toad) in kindergarten. She spent the rest of her school years with her nose in a book, pulling it out just long enough to earn a Bachelor of Arts degree in English Literature at Penn State University. Following graduation, she worked at several different publishing companies, learning about the day-to-day details of writing and producing books. After fifteen years of helping other writers realize their dreams, she decided that it was time to become a published writer herself. Since then she has written more than seventy books for young readers on topics including dinosaurs, dolphins, occupations, American history, ancient cultures, and ancient myths. Ms. Schomp lives in the Catskill Mountain region of New York, where she enjoys hiking, gardening, watching old movies on TV and new anime online, and, of course, reading, reading, and reading.